Introdu<

The Rhinog mountains form the disti
    the left of the A470 when you emerg
travelling north. Although not as high a
north, the Rhinogs nevertheless constitu
Snowdonia. The scenery is spectacular and, because there are no roads over
the ridge, the area surrounding this has retained its remoteness. Indeed, as a
result of its bronze age sites, medieval roads and houses, gold and manganese
mines, even wild goats, the area has a sense of mystery which is unique in
Wales.

The walks described here are concentrated to the east, with some walks to
the north and south, of the main Rhinog ridge since walks on the coastal side
of it are explored in other books in this series. The walks are readily
accessible from Bronaber and Trawsfynydd, while the larger centres of
Dolgellau and Porthmadog are a short distance away using the A470 or a
combination of the A487 and A470.

Any of these walks can be undertaken by a reasonably fit person with
Walks **3–5**, **10**, **16** and **18** being the most challenging and requiring good
visibility when attempted. Walking boots or strong shoes are recommended
for all of them. Please remember that the walks pass through sheep farming
country in which *dogs must be kept permanently on a lead.*

The location of each route is shown on the back cover and a summary of
the main characteristics and approximate length of each is shown on a chart.
An estimated duration is also given but it is best to allow longer in order to
linger over the many fine views and interesting places visited whilst on the
walks. Each walk has a map and description which enables the route to be
followed without further help. However, remember to take account of
weather conditions before setting out and dress accordingly, especially if you
intend to explore one of the higher routes. A weather forecast for this area is
available on 09068 232785 (charge) or at www.met-office.gov.uk.

About the author, Michael Burnett...
Michael is a musician who has written articles and presented radio
programmes about Welsh traditional music. His links to Wales go back to
his teenage years when he regularly stayed with friends near Maentwrog
and to the 1970s when he lived with his wife, Paula, and their two young
children at Blaen Myherin, a remote farmhouse above Devil's Bridge which
has now, sadly, become a ruin. Today Michael and Paula share an old
farmhouse near the northern Rhinog ridge.

WALK I

NANT PASGAN FROM TALLIN

DESCRIPTION This walk takes you across grassy fields and moorland from the old farmhouse of Tallin to Nant Pasgan Mawr, a medieval house set in an idyllic valley. Allow two hours.

START Parking space about ½-mile past Tyn y Ffridd (SH 648381)

DIRECTIONS From its junction with the A487 at Maentwrog take the A496 towards Harlech. At the crossroads in Llandecwyn, take the minor road opposite the tollbridge road from Penrhyndeudraeth and go uphill through the village. Continue until you reach a telephone box outside a former chapel. Turn LEFT here, go over a cattle-grid and bear RIGHT as you pass the lake of Tecwyn Isaf. Ignore the next right turn, going uphill and over another cattle-grid before passing Tyn y Ffridd on your left. After another ½-mile the road turns sharply right, going steeply uphill. On this bend a track goes off to the left past a permissive footpath sign. Park on the level grassy space on the right of the track.

1 Return to the road and go LEFT uphill. Take the first road on the RIGHT, where there is a sign for Tallin, and continue uphill. Just past some outbuildings, turn sharp LEFT by a telegraph post and take the track leading to a metal gate. *Before you turn look for Tallin farmhouse down to the right and catch a spectacular view out to sea over the Dwyryd Estuary.* Go through the gate and follow the winding track to a junction where a wall comes down from the right. *There is soon a view of the distinctive outlines of Moel Ysgyfarnogod and Foel Penolau (see* **Walk 3)** *above you to the right.* Bear LEFT here and soon go through a gateway in a wall. *Just past this there is a curved section of wall and you will see Llyn Llenyrch on your left. The lake is six acres in area and contains small trout.*

2 Follow the track downhill bearing RIGHT, through one stream and then, bearing LEFT, across another, before going gently uphill to the LEFT. After this, follow the track gently down to some rocky outcrops above which is another short stretch of wall. Bear sharp RIGHT just next to the first outcrop and below the wall. Make for the metal gate in the wall which is now ahead of you, keeping the gate in sight as the track becomes less clear. *From the gate you can see part of the roof and one of the chimneys of Nant Pasgan Mawr, over to the left.*

3 Go through the gate, crossing a boggy patch as you make for a gorse-covered hillock ahead of you. Go up on to the hillock and then bear half LEFT, through a tumbledown wall, across some bog and a stream, to a second metal gate. Beyond this, go ahead through reeds to some rocks. Ignoring the stile over to the right at this point, bear LEFT following a faint track which goes gently uphill, soon bearing RIGHT past a small tree which is rooted in the rocks to a gap in a wall. Go through and RIGHT to reach Nant Pasgan Mawr. *This farmhouse was described by architect Clough Williams-Ellis as the most beautiful medieval building in Gwynedd. Note the comparative smallness of the stones from which it is built, the shape of the door arch and the height of its chimneys. The house is well sited, high above the fast-flowing Nant Ddu and protected from the winds by the Rhinog ridge which it faces and the rocky outcrops which crouch behind it. Nant Pasgan Mawr is well preserved although lived-in for only short periods of the year.*

4 From the front of the house go alongside its left-hand wall to reach the track which runs behind it. Turn LEFT and through a gate to follow the track alongside those rocky outcrops. Soon another track comes in between the rocks on the RIGHT; ignore this for now although you will return to it later. Continue ahead following the track as it bends RIGHT to reach Nant Pasgan Bach. *Again beautifully situated, this less ancient farmhouse once had extensive*

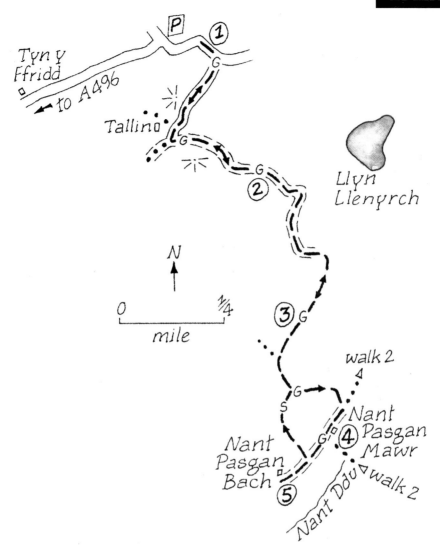

outbuildings to judge by the ruins facing it. And, from its rear, there is a good view down the valley towards Llandecwyn.

5 Return the short distance along the track to the junction mentioned earlier and turn LEFT to go through a wall (look for the radio mast on the distant hilltop ahead of you at this point). Go down a grassy slope making for a yellow footpath sign across the shallow valley ahead of you. Cross the bridge over a stream by the sign to go uphill in the direction of the arrow, passing the remains of a stone enclosure on the left. Bear RIGHT, watching for a rock perched on a hillock to the right. Continue ahead, in the direction of a large electricity pylon in the distance, and you will soon see a fence ahead of you. Make for a stile over the fence and turn LEFT to go down to the second of the metal gates you went through earlier. Retrace your steps from here back to the starting point.

WALK 2

NANT PASGAN FROM TYN TWLL

DESCRIPTION A varied walk which crosses the northern end of the Rhinog ridge and follows an ancient track down the austerely beautiful Cwm Moch. The objective of the walk is the remote farmhouse of Nant Pasgan Mawr, one of the best preserved medieval buildings in Gwynedd. Allow four hours.

START Parking space beside the footpath sign just to the north of the farm of Tyn Twll (SH 684358).

DIRECTIONS From the A470 just south of Trawsfynydd take the minor road which goes west towards the Rhinog ridge. Bear RIGHT after about a mile and continue for another mile to pass Tyn Twll which is on the right.

I Go through the metal gate next to the footpath sign and follow the track uphill. Soon another gate, with stile to the left, is reached. Pass through and make for another stile and gate to the RIGHT. Follow the path as it bears LEFT uphill parallel with a tumbledown wall. Go through another gate, with stile, continuing uphill through rocks and then across two streams and some bog. The path then reaches firmer ground and follows the wall uphill. *Trawsfynydd Nuclear Power Station can be seen to the east from here. This, the only inland nuclear site in the country, was built in the 1950s.* Bear RIGHT through a rocky gully to reach a gate.

2 After the gate, follow the path which bears slightly to the RIGHT and crosses the lowest point of the ridge. *There is a spectacular view to the west from here. It includes Cardigan Bay, Porthmadog, Yr Eifl. Moel Hebog and the Nantlle Ridge.* At this point, divert from the original track, which descends into a large bog, following a path which contours round to the LEFT. Pass a group of stones forming a cairn, one of several Bronze Age sites in this area, cross a stream and rejoin the track which descends

into Cwm Moch. Cross the stone-flag bridge over a stream and walk towards a low rock ridge ahead of you. Then bear RIGHT and make for the wall and stile on the hillside to the west. The path then passes through heather between a fence and a wall on the right.

3 Soon go through a gap in the wall to follow a fainter track which descends, passing a derelict wall on the left and going LEFT down to the remains of a barn. *From here the Pasgan Valley can be seen below and, in the distance, the Dwyryd estuary and Portmeirion.* Go LEFT through the gap in the wall just before the barn following the path through some bog before it becomes firmer on the descent to Nant Pasgan. *Soon the valley's two houses come into view, Nant Pasgan Bach to the left and the medieval Nant Pasgan Mawr to the right.* When a wall comes in from the left turn to the RIGHT, go down alongside the wall, bear LEFT, passing a ruined barn. Follow the path down and cross the slab bridge to reach the house.

4 At the house turn RIGHT towards a bridge over the river. *The impressive rocky hump of Manod Mawr, above Llan Ffestiniog, can be clearly seen to the east from here.* Ignore the bridge and keep to the LEFT of the river, following a faint path past some rocky humps to a single slab bridge. Ignore this, keeping to the LEFT of the river

4

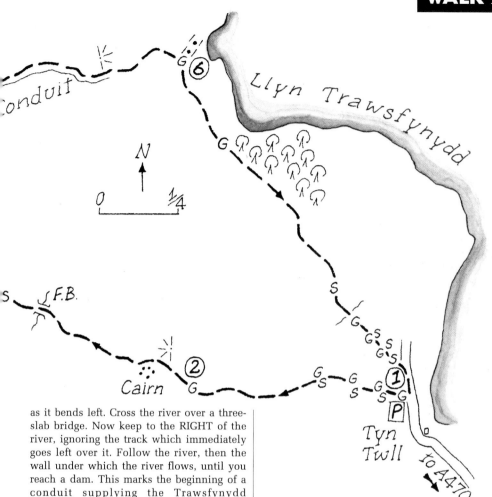

as it bends left. Cross the river over a three-slab bridge. Now keep to the RIGHT of the river, ignoring the track which immediately goes left over it. Follow the river, then the wall under which the river flows, until you reach a dam. This marks the beginning of a conduit supplying the Trawsfynydd reservoir.

5 Follow the path on the LEFT of the conduit, passing a bridge and a second dam. For a time the conduit goes undergound but the path remains clear, leading to a stile with a green marker. Soon the path becomes a track, bending away from the conduit. *The Trawsfynydd Lake dam can now be seen. To the right the rocky ridges of the end of the Rhinogs dominate the scene.* Soon the track rejoins the conduit, at which point turn sharp RIGHT behind a hillock for a gate with a yellow sign. (Check for a concrete building to the left and overhead electricity wires as markers for the turn.)

6 Go through the gate following a winding path though some boggy ground, across a stream, under the electricity wires and down to another gateway. Go through and uphill with wall to the left and wires to the right. Cross a ridge, descend under the wires and go over a stile. Soon there's a gate just over a stream, followed by another gate, marked 'private', with a stile to its right. Cross this stile, and then another, and follow the track downhill parallel to a wall on the left, ignoring the well-made track above you. After another stile you reach a road. Turn RIGHT and follow this back to your car.

WALK 3
MOEL YSGYFARNOGOD

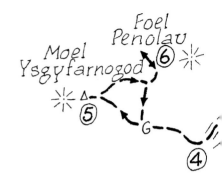

DESCRIPTION This dramatic walk climbs through old manganese workings to reach the summit of Moel Ysgyfarnogod with its spectacular views of the Dwyryd estuary and Snowdonia. On the return you visit the twin rocky summits of Foel Penolau just north of Ysgyfarnogod along the Rhinog ridge. Allow 3½ hours.

START Parking space on mine workings on the left of the road about ½ mile below the farm of Cefn Clawdd (SH 684336).

DIRECTIONS From the A470 just south of Trawsfynydd take the minor road which goes west towards the Rhinog ridge. Bear LEFT after about a mile and continue for 1½ miles, going through a gate and passing two tracks off to the LEFT. The second track has a footpath sign and just past it you will see a fenced-off mine shaft entrance on the RIGHT and the levelled-off mine workings opposite. Park here.

1 Walk up the road towards Cefn Clawdd and take a track off to the RIGHT just before the farm, passing under a low electricity wire. Keep to the stone-based track which goes uphill near a wall on the left, through which are the ruins of the original Cefn Clawdd. After about 10 minutes go through a wooden gate, by which time the track, built to facilitate access to the old Cefn Clawdd manganese mines, is firm and clear. Pass through a second gate, this time metal, and follow the track round the hillside and into the cwm below the rocky summit of Foel Penolau. *There is a good view, to the left from here, of Bwlch Gwylim, one of the four main passes over the Rhinog ridge. A track goes over the bwlch to Cwm Bychan.*

2 Soon a small forestry plantation comes into sight to the right ahead and the track goes through a low wall and across a stream, followed by a boggy patch, to reach the first of the Cefn Clawdd manganese workings.

The remains of a substantial mine building can be seen and the low spoil heaps have the feel of ancient ramparts. The discovery that manganese helped strengthen steel resulted in 12 mines being opened in Meirionnydd during 1886 alone. Yet, during 1892, the ten men working at Llyn Du Bach mine, just below Moel Ysgyfarnogod, failed to extract a single ton of manganese at this exposed ridge-top site. Most of the mines were closed within a few years.

3 The track continues uphill, bending round to the LEFT before ending next to some lengths of the original metal tram lines. *Looking to the south and east at this point there is an impressive view of the Crawcwellt, a large area of marshland which drains into the river Eden (see* **Walk 8***). Much of this land has recently been made a Site of Special Scientific Interest as it provides a habitat unique in Britain for a variety of plant and animal species.* Continue ahead, following a faint path on your RIGHT through the heather and rocks, and avoiding a boggy patch, to reach a tumbledown wall.

4 Turning RIGHT, go through this and walk up the grass and heather slope, making for the gap in the wall which can be seen above. Go through the gap (there is a wooden gate here but it is usually lying on the ground) where the ground is very muddy. Go across to the small ridge on your LEFT and follow another faint path which goes uphill on it. Soon, pass through two rocky outcrops to reach the ridge and then walk up to the summit on the LEFT, where there is a triangulation station. *The view from here is excellent, with Snowdon towering to the north, the Dwyryd Estuary, with the Italianate village of Portmeirion conspicuous on its far shore, below you, and Cardigan Bay stretching as far as the eye can*

summit, which is separated from you by a deep gully, return part of the way you have just some, then scramble LEFT down into the gully. Then go up through boulders and rock slabs to reach the second summit. *Due to its rocks and cliffs, Foel Penolau has the feel of a much higher, less easily accessible mountain and the view from it is, again, magnificent. Look to the east and you will see another mountain with twin peaks, Arenig Fawr, and, beyond that, to the south-east, the ridge of the Arans.*

③ ②

G ─ G

N

0 ¼

Cefn Clawdd

Mine workings to A470

① P

see. A short walk to the western summit of Ysgyfarnogod opens up more views of the estuary.

5 Leave the summit of Moel Ysgyfarnogod making for the rocky peak of Foel Penolau to the north-east. Keep RIGHT, aiming for the right-hand end of the cliffs facing you, where they are joined by a wall. Once there clamber over the jumble of rocks and then bear LEFT, going up a rock and grass covered slope to reach the first summit of Foel Penolau. To get to the northern

6 Return to the gully, bear LEFT and then RIGHT to go back down to the wall adjoining the cliffs at the southern end of Foel Penolau. From here, follow the wall downhill, keeping to the RIGHT of it until you reach the gap you came through earlier. Then retrace your steps to your car.

Moel Ysgyfarnogod and Foel Penolau from above Cefn Clawdd

WALK 4

CLIP

DESCRIPTION This wild walk takes you through Bwlch Gwylim, high on the Rhinog ridge, to the spectacular rock-pavement summit of Clip. This little-known mountain top has cliffs on three sides and provides excellent views of Cwm Bychan, the coast near Shell Island and of Cardigan Bay. Allow 3½ hours.

START Parking space on mine workings on the left of the road about ½ mile below the farm of Cefn Clawdd (SH 684336).

DIRECTIONS From the A470 just south of Trawsfynydd take the minor road which goes west towards the Rhinog ridge. Bear LEFT after about a mile and continue for 1½ miles, going through a gate and passing two tracks off to the LEFT. The second track has a footpath sign and just past it you will see a fenced-off mine shaft entrance on the RIGHT and the levelled-off mine workings opposite. Park here.

towards the house you can see up the valley. Go through a gateway and walk alongside the house on its RIGHT. *This isolated house is identified on the map as Wern Cyfrdwy although named Wern Uchaf on the door. The attractive arched footbridge over the river in front of the house was built recently.*

2 Go uphill from the far end of the house, crossing a boggy patch and through a gateway. Keeping quite close to the river and wall on your right, make your way towards the distant ridge ahead, crossing the first of a number of small drainage ditches and negotiating muddy sections of a faint path. Note when the wall alongside the river on the right is replaced with a fence but continue ahead, making for the lower part of a wall which goes up the valley to the left.

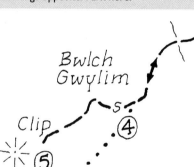

Bear slightly RIGHT towards the point where the fence next to what is now a stream on your right is replaced with an initially tumbledown wall. Then bear slightly LEFT, going uphill alongside the stream and wall. Soon cross the stream where it cuts across the line of the path but continue uphill with the stream on your left and the wall on your right. Cross the stream again and bear LEFT uphill making for a stile across the wall which comes in at right angles to the wall you are alongside.

I Return to the track with the footpath sign and turn RIGHT. Follow the track until it divides just before a telegraph pole with a yellow marker. Go LEFT here, cross a footbridge over the Afon Crawcwellt and go over the stile by the uninhabited farm of Wern Fach. Turn RIGHT and make for a stile you can see ahead of you. Once over, go ahead, crossing a stream and then a second stile near a second bridge over the Crawcwellt. *There is a good view from here of Moel Ysgyfarnogod and the rocky Foel Penolau high above you to the right (see* **Walk 3***).* Go ahead, following a muddy path

3 Cross the stile (there is an old sheep gathering pen to the right of it and a gateway through the wall to its left). Continue uphill, following the path across a stream and some bog before it climbs, more steeply now, through rocks and heather with the wall coming up from the valley still on the right. Then, as you get higher, the path goes RIGHT to join the wall and takes you uphill next to it. When the wall bends away to the right and goes up on to the ridge above you continue ahead into an increasingly narrow gully. Soon, cross a stream and keep to the RIGHT of a level boggy patch. The path then goes through heather, next to a stream, making for the summit of the pass, a rocky knoll which you can see above you. Just before the knoll, bear RIGHT at a junction of paths and go uphill to pass the summit on your left. Here, bear RIGHT again, and make for a stile over a wall.

4 Cross the stile, and go steeply uphill until you reach the ridge. Turn LEFT, joining a path which takes you into a rocky gully. Scramble up this and then follow the ridge, making for the cairn on the next high point, which is Clip. Drop down, bearing slightly RIGHT, then go LEFT and RIGHT up a narrow gully near the left end of the cliff below the cairn. *The summit ridge of Clip provides contrasting views. Southwards, the barren rocks and cliffs of the Rhinogs stretch majestically into the distance, while, from the large cairn at the western end of the ridge, idyllic Cwm Bychan, and parts of the comparatively lush coastal plain, can be seen.*

5 Re-trace your steps via Bwlch Gwylim and Wern Uchaf to your car. *An alternative return can be made by following the northern Rhinog ridge to the summit of Moel Ysgyfarnogod, then re-tracing sections **4–1** of **Walk 3**. However, paths are unreliable on this part of the ridge and misty conditions can befuddle even the most experienced of walkers.*

Wern Uchaf

9

RHINOG FAWR

DESCRIPTION This walk takes you to Bwlch Tyddiad, the high pass over the Rhinog ridge through which runs the partly paved trackway known as the Roman Steps, before skirting the remote Llyn Du to ascend the steep slopes of the highest of the two Rhinog peaks. This summit is a dominant feature of the area and an unrivalled viewpoint. Allow 4½ hours.

START Parking space just inside the forest near Graigddu Isaf (SH 684302).

DIRECTIONS From the A470 about ½-mile south of Bronaber take the unsignposted minor road heading west towards the Rhinog ridge. Go through a gate and over a bridge and cattle-grid. The road winds through moorland to a gate next to the forest below the Rhinogs. Go through and park on the LEFT.

I Bear LEFT to follow a track into the forest which runs parallel with a fence on your RIGHT. Soon, go ahead on a path next to a blue marker. Cross four bridges over small streams, remaining parallel with the fence on the right. As the trees thin out bear gently LEFT on the path and cross another stream making for a blue marker by a bridge. Turn LEFT onto the track here, across the bridge and through the gate beyond it. *The buildings you are passing belong to the farm of Graigddu Isaf over to the right.* Follow the track until you reach a blue National Park notice where you should take the path going off to the RIGHT. Ignore a path going left next to a yellow marker and continue alongside a stream on the right, going uphill through some bog and past a waterfall (Pistyll Gwyn). Continue ahead until you reach a forestry track which crosses the path at right angles.

2 Go over the track and follow the path over two footbridges to reach the edge of the forest. There is a wooden gate here and, beyond it, a Countryside Council for Wales notice confirming that you are entering the Rhinog Nature Reserve. *Pause here for a moment to take in the view of the rocky*

slopes and summit of Rhinog Fawr to your left and the summit of the pass ahead. In winter, the wild goats which inhabit this region may sometimes be seen between this

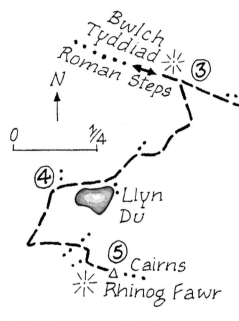

point and the summit. Follow the path as it winds uphill through some patches of bog, past another Nature Reserve sign and over some rock-slab paving – a precursor of the Roman Steps – for part of the way. Ignore a path going off to the left for the moment and continue to the top of the pass to admire the view east and west. *The Roman Steps is an accurate term in that a trackway probably passed through Bwlch Tyddiad in Roman times. However the wide stone slabs which gave rise to the name are likely to be of medieval origin and put in place as part of a pack-horse trail. A short walk downhill to the west from the summit will bring you to sections of paving.*

3 Return a short distance downhill to take the path, now going off to the RIGHT, which you saw earlier. Follow this uphill through heather and boulders, ignoring a path coming in from the left, until you reach Llyn Du. *This isolated lake is in an impressive rock ampitheatre and contains* *small trout. It is four acres in area.* Follow the path to the rocks on the RIGHT of the lake and then scramble over the rocks alongside it to rejoin the path at the far end

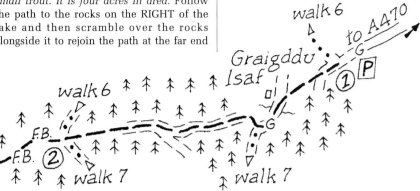

of the lake. Continue ahead, making for a wall coming downhill from the left.

4 Turn LEFT when you reach the wall and go alongside it uphill. Soon bear RIGHT through a gap in the wall to go up alongside a second wall. Keep to the left of this, ignoring a path going off to the left. After some ups and downs, bear half-LEFT away from the wall at the point at which the path is level with the top of it. Go LEFT to follow the path uphill, ignoring any other paths going left, to reach a small cairn. Bear LEFT here on the path, ignoring another path on the right, to go upwards on a stone ridge. When a path joins yours from the left, bear RIGHT towards the scree slope you can see above. Continue ahead, ignoring a path on the right, past another small cairn and then immediately bear RIGHT (do not go ahead at this important junction). Follow the path which leads over to the scree and up

through the gully above it. The summit is a short distance from the top of the gully. *There are two large cairns at the summit of Rhinog Fawr which offers panoramic views. Cardigan Bay and the Lleyn Peninsula stretch out to the west, Snowdon towers to the north, Arenig and the Arans dominate the view to the east, and Cadair Idris can be seen to the south. Nearer at hand is Rhinog Fach, whose slopes encircle tiny Llyn Cwmhosan, and, below to the north-west, Cwm Bychan.*

5 Return to the gully and retrace your steps via Llyn Du, Bwlch Tyddiad and Graigddu Isaf to the starting point of the walk. *It is possible to return by making your way southwards from Rhinog Fawr down to Bwlch Drws Ardudwy and then following* **Walk 7**, *sections* **3** *and* **4**. *However, path finding is difficult above the pass and there are many steep cliffs and confusing gullies.*

Rhinog Fawr from the east

NORTH OF RHINOG FAWR

DESCRIPTION A fascinating walk which climbs gently up to Hafod Gynfal, a ruined farmhouse near the northern Rhinog ridge, and provides spectacular views of the whole area. The views were obscured by conifers until recently when this part of the forest was felled and re-planted. Allow 2½ hours.

START Parking space just inside the forest near Graigddu Isaf (SH 684302).

DIRECTIONS From the A470 about ½-mile south of Bronaber take the unsignposted minor road heading west towards the Rhinog ridge. Go through a gate and over a bridge and cattle-grid. The road winds through moorland to a gate next to the forest below the Rhinogs. Go through and park on the LEFT.

1 Follow the track into the forest to the RIGHT and take the first RIGHT, going uphill through a wooden gate with a yellow marker on it. After the gate bear RIGHT again, cross a stream and go out of the trees, continuing uphill. Go ahead where a track crosses, at a footpath sign, and pass, on the left, a white arrow pointing ahead. *If you pause here and look behind you there is a good view, left, to Y Garn (see* **Walk 18***), an outlying peak of the Rhinogs, and, ahead, in the distance, the ridge of Cadair Idris.* The track bears round to the LEFT, passing another white arrow. Watch for a wall coming down to the track on the right next to a yellow arrow on the left.

2 Here, go to the RIGHT uphill, past yellow and white arrows, to reach the wall and a yellow arrow. Go LEFT here and soon go RIGHT through a gap in the wall, ignoring the yellow arrow further uphill. Pass three wooden posts with green-painted tops to reach Hafod Gynfal. Go alongside its right-hand wall to reach the entrance to this ruined farmhouse. *Hafod Gynfal is a casualty of the Forestry Commission's early view that the land it purchased should be used exclusively for conifer plantation. Many farmhouses throughout Wales were, like Hafod Gynfal, emptied of their occupants and left to rot amidst impenetratable ranks of evergreens. Gynfal was quite a large house and built into the hillside. Note the large fireplace here, with a small alcove on its right, and the section of railway line used as a beam. Go uphill from the front of the house to the yellow marker. This is a good place for a picnic, with plenty of tree-stumps to sit on, and there is an excellent all-round view, from the Arenigs in the north to Cadair Idris in the south.*

3 Return to Hafod Gynfal, then back down to the forestry track and turn RIGHT. *You can see, from this section of track, the steep cliffs on the northern ridge of the Rhinogs ahead.* Soon the track bears LEFT, downhill, passing some ruined sheep-pens on the left. Pass another white arrow, on the left, and go over a concrete bridge. *Stop at the next white arrow to admire the precipices of Rhinog Fach which is directly ahead of you at this point.* Pass more sheep-pens on the right and then two more white arrows *(Rhinog Fawr is now directly ahead).* Soon the track falls to a bridge over the Nant Llyn Du next to some footpath signs. Go over the bridge and turn LEFT.

For section **4** of this walk follow section **4** of **Walk 7**.

WALK 7

BELOW THE RHINOGS

DESCRIPTION A walk which takes you into the pass between the two Rhinog peaks, Bwlch Drws Ardudwy. On the way you enter an area designated a National Nature Reserve and may well see the goats which roam wild in these precipitous mountains. Allow 2½ hours.

START See **Walk 6**

DIRECTIONS See **Walk 6**

I Bear LEFT to follow a track into the forest which runs parallel with a fence on your RIGHT. Soon, go ahead on a path next to a blue marker. Cross four bridges over small streams, remaining parallel with the fence on the right. As the trees thin out bear gently LEFT on the path and cross another stream making for a blue marker by a bridge. Turn LEFT onto the track here, across the bridge and through the gate beyond it. *The farm buildings you are passing belong to Graigddu Isaf. Several of its neighbours, including Hafod Gynfal (see* **Walk 6***), become derelict after the land was taken over by the Forestry Commission for conifer plantation.* Follow the track, passing a blue National Park notice and path going off to the right. Bear RIGHT when the track divides and go through a gate uphill. Ignoring turnings to the right, continue until the track bends LEFT to go over a bridge.

2 Here, bear RIGHT to go uphill alongside a stream. At the forest edge go through a gate into the Rhinog Nature Reserve. Follow the obvious

path, soon noting a path going to the right, which you will take later. Shortly you will arrive at the summit of the pass which is marked by a cairn. *Watch for the wild goats, and also for the ravens, which inhabit this wild spot beneath the towering ramparts of the two Rhinogs.*

3 Return to the junction of paths and bear LEFT. Go uphill initially and then down to a fence and stile next to the forest. Go over, then RIGHT over another stile into the forest. The path is muddy but easy to follow. Turn LEFT when you reach a forestry track and follow it until you reach a signpost just before a bridge. Turn RIGHT here.

4 After turning off the forestry track follow a path alongside the stream on your LEFT. Pass a waterfall and follow the path through trees to a yellow marker. Bear LEFT here and follow the path to a blue National Park notice. Turn LEFT onto a forestry track, going through a gate and over a bridge next to Graigddu Isaf. Go RIGHT at a blue arrow, cross a stream and follow a path into the trees, crossing four bridges over small streams to reach a forestry track and blue arrow. Keep LEFT to join the track which leads back to your car.

Hafod Gynfal ③

② Walk 6

N

F.B.

0 ¼ mile

Graigddu Isaf ①P to A470

walk 5 ④

Walk 7

Rhinog Fawr

Cairn ③

Bwlch Drws Ardudwy

Rhinog Fach

②

WALK 8

HEAD OF THE EDEN

DESCRIPTION A gentle walk which takes you through the mixture of moorland and sheep pasture surrounding the headwaters of the River Eden. It provides good views of the Rhinog ridge and passes Maesgwm, a large old house overlooking Coed y Brenin, the forest park which has been developed as a mountain-biking centre. Allow 1½ hours.

START Parking space just across the River Eden from Gelli Goch (SH 710290).

DIRECTIONS From the A470 about two miles south of Bronaber take the unsignposted minor road heading west. There is a gateway between walls at the entrance to the road which you should follow downhill to a junction. Bear RIGHT here, go over the bridge and park a short distance beyond it on the wide verge on the RIGHT next to a barn and footpath sign.

I Walk along the road, going over a bridge which crosses a gorge containing the tumbling waters of the Afon Crawcwellt and then through a farm gate. *You are now entering a large area of marshy grassland, which stretches from Trawsfynydd Lake in the north to here, called the Crawcwellt. The area is unique for its animal and plant life, and parts of it have recently been made a Site of Special Scientific Interest (SSSI) for this reason. The two main rivers which drain the marshland, north and south, flow eastwards from the Rhinog ridge and are each called Crawcwellt until they join the Eden. The Eden itself is part of the SSSI for its entire length (ie. until it flows into the Afon Mawddach at Ganllwyd). Its head waters contain the last breeding population of freshwater pearl mussel in Wales and are home to Atlantic salmon, water voles and otters.* The road climbs, revealing the Rhinog peaks ahead, and soon reaches the gate leading into the farm of Ffridd Bryn Coch.

2 Go ahead, making for a stile with a white arrow next to it. Go over this and walk alongside a corrugated iron barn before bearing LEFT through a metal gate. Follow the track, going parallel with a rebuilt wall on the left and ignoring a gate in it. Go over a stile alongside a gate, continuing ahead across the field towards a barn then bearing to the RIGHT just before it. Cross a stream and make for two stiles which are next to each other. Cross the stile on the RIGHT, and go straight ahead, ignoring a metal gate down to the left, through a boggy patch and over two streams to cross a stile at the end of a wall.

3 Keeping to the right-hand edge of the grassy field make for a wooden gate in the wall ahead, to the right of the large house (Aber Serw) you can see. Go through, across a track and over a footbridge to join a tarmac road going ahead (south). Follow the road and go through a wooden gate. Then turn RIGHT through a smaller wooden gate and go uphill on a path leading to the buildings above you. Skirt these, going below them to reach a surfaced track. *The large house and outbuildings you have reached is Maesgwm, an old settlement perched high above the Eden valley and the now afforested slopes which have taken its name. Those living here only 20 years ago would, no doubt, have been astonished to see the helmetted, lycra-clad cyclists who regularly dash past the door of Maesgwm today, seeking thrills on the trails provided for them in Coed y Brenin.*

4 Go LEFT downhill on the track, through a gateway to a junction, then turn LEFT onto a tarmac road. *Turn RIGHT if you would like to follow the road the short distance down to the Maesgwm Centre where there is a café, shop and display giving information on the locality.* Go ahead, passing the gate you went through on your way up to Maesgwm house and then going through the gate across the road. Go over the footbridge, across the track leading to Aber Serw and then through the gate ahead. Go in the direction indicated by the yellow arrow there, keeping to the edge of the field. Make for a metal gate on the far side of it, passing a pile of boulders and stones on your right. Go

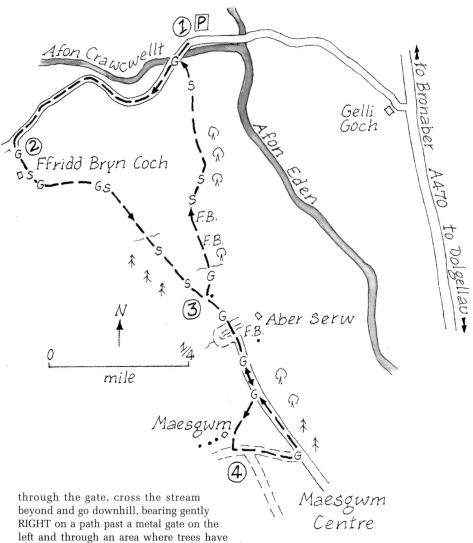

through the gate, cross the stream beyond and go downhill, bearing gently RIGHT on a path past a metal gate on the left and through an area where trees have recently been planted. Go over a small bridge, through some tussocky bog and then over another bridge. Bear LEFT, then half-RIGHT, and make for a group of tall trees ahead. Go under the trees then follow the path half-LEFT towards a wall and, just before this, a fence and stile. Go over the stile, bear RIGHT and then, after a short distance, cross a second stile where there is a white marker post on the right. Ignore the

direction indicated by the marker and go ahead keeping close to a wall on the left and making for a stile across the wall ahead of you. Cross the stile and the track beyond it, then go ahead uphill to the metal gate you can see. Turn RIGHT onto the road you reach, go through the gate and return to your car.

15

DOLDDINAS

DESCRIPTION This fascinating walk visits the ruined settlement of Dolddinas and passes remote Llyn Hiraethlyn before joining the track of the disused Bala to Blaenau Ffestiniog railway. Allow two and a half hours. **Note that the ford at Dolddinas can become impassable after heavy rain.**

START Parking space beside the minor road to Bwlch Gwyn Uchaf from the A4212 (SH 726362).

DIRECTIONS From the A470 as it bypasses Trawsfynydd take the A4212 heading towards Bala. Pass a road on the left signposted 'Stesion' and, about a mile from the A470, take the minor road on the LEFT opposite a footpath sign. Go over a cattle-grid and park where the road widens after about 400m.

I Follow the road north to Bwlch Gwyn Uchaf and continue on the unmetalled track to go over a low ridge before reaching the Llafar valley. Bear RIGHT at a blue notice banning motorised traffic on Mynydd Maentwrog. *This is now Crown Estate land although there has been mining activity here in the past, at Braich Ddu slate quarry and Prince Edward gold mine. Gold from the latter was used in the regalia for the investiture of the Prince of Wales in 1911.* Follow the track alongside a wall on the right, passing a ruined outbuilding. Soon you reach a junction next to the ruined farmhouse of Dolddinas. *Facing you here is a slate-roofed privy built, typically, over a stream. The track past Dolddinas follows the Roman road Sarn Helen (see **Walk 13**) and there are the rectangular earthworks of three Roman practice camps just to the north of the house.*

2 Bear RIGHT at Dolddinas, going down to the river and a wooden gate. Follow the fence along to the right of the gate to where it crosses the Llafar. Ford the river and cross the fence using the stile facing you. Turn LEFT, walking parallel to the river before

making gently uphill for a wooden gate. Go through to cross a spur from the hillside on the right. Pass through two rocky outcrops and follow a faint path round to the RIGHT, keeping above the stream to your left. Continue uphill, going RIGHT through a grassy gully. The path goes down, half-LEFT, to a small metal gate and a stile. Go through and uphill to join a path going south. Soon you will see Llyn Hiraethlyn, down to the right, as you make for a gateway ahead. The track then climbs to the left of the lake. *From the top of the next rise you can see, to the south, Moel Oernant (see **Walk 10**) and Craiglaseithin (**Walk 11**). Llyn Hiraethlyn is 11 acres in area and was known for a unique breed of perch with a twisted tail. The lake's name – 'The lake of longing' – derives from a legend describing how a young man, grieving at the death of his beloved, attempts to cross the lake when it is frozen. However, the springs which emerge at the lake's centre have thinned the ice which breaks beneath the young man, causing him to drown. There is a smaller Llyn Hiraethlyn two miles away near the summit of Moel Oernant.*

3 Follow the track as it bears LEFT before going through a wall ahead. The track winds downhill, crossing a stream before reaching a wooden gate and stile, and then going down to the disused Bala-Blaenau Ffestiniog railway line. Bear RIGHT, under the line, and then LEFT, following the track uphill. Turn LEFT onto the line to meet the first of several combined gateways and stiles. *You are now west of the site of Bryncelynog Halt on the Bala-Blaenau Ffestiniog line. This section was opened by the Great Western Railway in 1882 and required the construction of 11 viaducts, of which the most impressive is at the head of Cwm Prysor. This can be reached from the parking space on the left of the A4212 at the top of the pass. Further along the A4212, on the right, Cwm Prysor station-house can still be seen.*

4 Follow the line through a short cutting and onto an embankment before you reach a second gate and style. The track goes over another bridge and into a deep, boggy

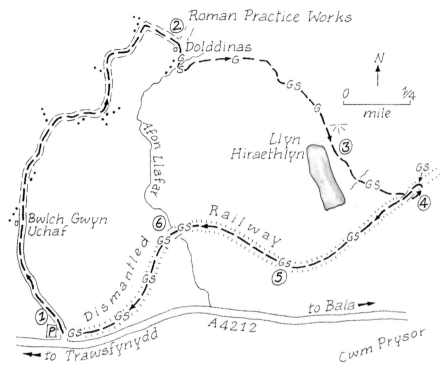

Roman Practice Works

Dolddinas

N

0 ——— ¼
mile

Llyn
Hiraethlyn

Afon Llafar

Bwlch Gwyn
Uchaf

Railway

Dismantled

to Trawsfynydd

A4212

to Bala →

Cwm Prysor

cutting. Here, go up to the LEFT to skirt the edge of the cutting. Return to the line, following it to a third gate and stile.

5 As the line widens skirt round to the LEFT at the point where it is blocked with trees. Then regain the line, passing the remains of a brick-built ganger's refuge. There are gates and stiles on each side of the magnificent bridge over the Llafar.

6 Soon after the bridge go briefly up to the LEFT to avoid a short boggy patch on the line. You will then pass two more gates and stiles, and through two low cuttings, before reaching the final gate and stile. Turn RIGHT on to the road beyond and follow it back to your car.

Dolddinas and the Roman practice camps from the air

WALK 10

MOEL OERNANT

DESCRIPTION A walk which takes you to a remote mountain top from which there is a panoramic view of the peaks and ridges of southern Snowdonia. Allow two and a half hours. *This walk should not be attempted in poor visibility as it depends upon the ability to make out specific features of the landscape at a distance.*

START Parking space at the end of the tarmac road up the Gain valley (SH 755336).

DIRECTIONS From the A470 at Bronaber, two miles south of Trawsfynydd, take the minor road signposted for Llanuwchllyn, Abergeirw and the Trawsfynydd holiday village. Bear LEFT at the entrance to the village, then LEFT again to cross a cattle-grid. Pass the entrance to the Rhiwgoch Inn and artificial ski slope on the right, continuing uphill to pass Pen y Stryd farm on the left. Cross a second cattle-grid, continuing ahead to pass a conifer plantation and go downhill. Bear LEFT at a junction, taking the road signposted Llanuwchllyn, and, soon, go over another cattle-grid. Ignore a road going off to the right and, when the Llanuwchllyn road turns sharp right to cross a bridge over the Afon Gain, go ahead past a dead-end sign. This road crosses the Gain and ends at a gate. Park on the LEFT of the road adjacent to the gate.

I Before leaving the parking space glance at the top of the steep bank on the opposite side of the River Gain. You will see a tall metal post near a short wooden one. The metal post is your first objective (Point **A**). Go back along the road to cross the bridge over the Gain and then go RIGHT to climb parallel to the river making first for the wooden post and then, when it comes into sight, the metal post. At the metal post turn LEFT and begin climbing the hillside, making for the rock-slab and grass covered summit on the ridge directly above you (Point **B**). The ascent takes you up the centre of a wide, tussocky grass-covered plateau between two streams. On the way you'll pass two large hollows which are quite likely

shell-holes, an often occurring legacy of the army's occupation of the Gain valley area (see **Walk 13**). As you get higher bear LEFT towards the stream there, passing a large boulder next to it. Go up close to the stream to reach the area of moorland which the stream drains, and continue upwards, still making for the rocky summit you can see above. Mark the summit's position and continue in its direction as it briefly goes out of sight, passing to the RIGHT of a lower rock and grass covered knoll. When the summit comes into sight again you will see, below it, the collapsing stone-built walls of some sheep pens. Make for these and then for the summit itself. *If you look back down to the starting point next to the River Gain from here you will see several circular, water-filled holes above its far bank. These are shell-holes, too.*

2 Once at the rocky summit bear RIGHT along the grassy ridge, passing a small cairn and, after a short distance, when the ridge drops down, turn LEFT to cross the tussocky grass making for a dip in the near hillside. As you go through the dip a small lake (Point **C**) comes into sight just below you. Bear RIGHT to skirt the edge of the lake and then LEFT to cross the boggy patch at its end. *The lake is known as Llyn Hiraethlyn-the lake of longing- and is at a height of 1500 feet. It has no fish, unlike its larger namesake (see **Walk 10**) which can be seen in the distance, on the far side of the Prysor Valley, from here.*

3 A fairly clear path goes uphill from this end of Llyn Hiraethlyn. Look for it, ahead of you, as you cross the boggy patch at this end the lake. Continue uphill following the ridge and soon you will see, over to the right, the summit of Moel Oernant with its triangulation station. Go ahead to the highest point of the ridge (and southern end of the summit ridge: Point **D**) and then turn RIGHT, passing the wooden base of a telegraph pole to reach the summit. *There is evidence of the army's use of the summit, both in the concrete base adjoining it and in the leaning telegraph post which can be seen at the northern end of the summit ridge. A line of*

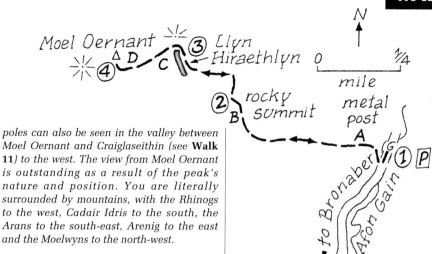

poles can also be seen in the valley between Moel Oernant and Craiglaseithin (see **Walk 11**) to the west. The view from Moel Oernant is outstanding as a result of the peak's nature and position. You are literally surrounded by mountains, with the Rhinogs to the west, Cadair Idris to the south, the Arans to the south-east, Arenig to the east and the Moelwyns to the north-west.

4 Retrace your steps to the starting point making, in turn, for Points **D** (southern end of summit ridge), **C** (Llyn Hiraethlyn), **B** (rock-slab and grass covered summit with small cairn) and **A** (metal post).

Translations

The following are translations of some important reference points in the walks:

Afon Hirgwm	River of the Long Valley
Bwlch Ardudwy	Doorway to Ardudwy. Ardudwy is the coastal region to the west of the Rhinog ridge and the bwlch is the pass between the two Rhinog summits (see below)
Clip	Short, sharp-edged hill
Craiglaseithin	Rock of Green Gorse. Gorse was once grown in the hills as cattle fodder
Crawcwellt	Area of Coarse Grass. This large region of grass and bog stretches from Trawsfynydd lake in the north to near Coed y Brenin in the south. It lies to the east of the Rhinog ridge and can be clearly seen from the A470
Diffwys	Precipice
Dolddinas	Field of the Fort. The reference to a fort is probably to the remains of the Roman practice camps which adjoin the ruined farmhouse of Dolddinas
Foel Penolau	Hill with a light bare top
Llyn Hiraethlyn	Lake of Longing
Llyn Llenyrch	Lake in a flat, open space
Maesgwm	Field of the Valley
Moel Oernant	Hill of the Cold Stream
Moel Ysgyfarnogod	Hill of the Hare
Rhinog Fach, Rhinog Fawr	Lower Threshold, Higher Threshold. The two Rhinogs are separated by Bwlch Ardudwy (see above) and thus together constitute the threshold to the coastal region beyond. Rhinog Fawr is the summit to the right of the bwlch, or pass, when looking from the east
Y Garn	The Cairn

CRAIGLASEITHIN

DESCRIPTION A walk which skirts an isolated moorland lake before reaching an easily attained peak with dramatic cliffs to the west. You are rewarded with spectacular views of the mountains of Snowdonia. Allow two hours.

START Parking space near the farmhouse of Pen y Stryd (SH 726318).

DIRECTIONS From the A470 at Bronaber, two miles south of Trawsfynydd, take the minor road signposted for Llanuwchllyn, Abergeirw and the Trawsfynydd holiday village. Bear LEFT at the entrance to the village, then LEFT again to cross a cattle-grid. Pass the entrance to the Rhiwgoch Inn and artificial ski slope on the right, continuing uphill to pass Pen y Stryd farm on the left. Bear RIGHT just past the farm, go over a second cattle-grid and park on the right-hand verge of the wide road junction.

1 Go over the cattle-grid and through the metal gate on the RIGHT to take the track which goes off to the RIGHT. Pass a fenced enclosure, going uphill to go over another cattle-grid and through a second metal gate. The track contours round the hill to the LEFT continuing uphill through a wall and across a boggy patch to reach another cattle-grid and makeshift gate. *The valley below you is that of the Afon Gain (see* **Walk 13***) and the mountain dominating the scene to the south-east is Rhobell Fawr. The track was built in 1941 by the water board and it passes several of the board's concrete markers.*

2 Soon you'll see a metal container on the left of the track and, ahead, the dam at Llyn Gelli Gain. Pass a wooden post with white and black depth markings next to the stream on your right as you walk to the dam. *From here, you can see the conical peak of your objective, Craiglaseithin.*

3 Once you reach the dam go to the RIGHT of it to skirt the eastern perimeter of the lake. *Llyn Gelli Gain is at a height of 1100 feet and was, until 1993, a reservoir*

supplying drinking water to the village of Trawsfynydd. The lake was once famous for its large eels. Now it contains pike weighing up to 8lbs. Keep to higher ground to avoid the boggy patches near the water's edge then, just after passing the remains of a stone hut on your right, drop down to the LEFT to cross the shallow gully at the eastern edge of the lake. Cross some rocks and then make uphill for the peak of Craiglaseithin which is directly ahead, following a faint path. Pass the remains of a building over to the right as the first slope levels off then make for the summit of Craiglaseithin, zig-zagging upwards between the rocks and boulders which litter the steep hillside. *The summit of Craiglaseithin became an observation post when the Gain valley area was used for manoeuvres by the army (see* **Walk 13***), the two metal posts on the summit being all that remains of the equipment which was placed here. The view is wide-ranging, taking in the peaks of Eryri, including Snowdon, to the north, the Rhinog Ridge to the west, Cadair Idris to the south, the Arans to the south-east, and Arenig to the east. The impressive hump of a mountain just to the east, higher than Craiglaseithin and with a triangulation station clearly visible on its summit, is Moel Oernant (see* **Walk 10***). The large lake to the north-west is Llyn Trawsfynydd, a reservoir which became the site of the only inland nuclear power station in Britain, also in sight, during the 1950s. The power station has been de-commissioned and is soon to be reduced in height and buried. The footbridge at the near end of the lake carries a path from the village of Trawsfynydd, and you can see the dam at the far north-western edge of the lake. Traws, as it is known locally, is worth a visit as it is much more attractive than it initially appears.*

4 After admiring the view zig-zag down from the summit making for the western-most (extreme RIGHT) edge of Llyn Gelli Gain where a faint track can be seen crossing a wet patch of ground. As you go, keep to higher ground on the left of the bog in the bottom of the valley. Then cross the stream which runs into the lake at its western-most point, using the stepping stones.

5 Go ahead to follow the western edge of the lake, keeping to higher ground so as to avoid the rough ground next to the water. At the southern end of this short, straight stretch of the lake go up higher. Then bear half LEFT from the corner of Llyn Gelli Gain, going gently uphill before making down for a ruined building. Pass to the RIGHT of this and then bear LEFT towards the post with its white and black markings next to the dam.

6 Having reached the post turn RIGHT onto the track and follow it back to the start of the walk.

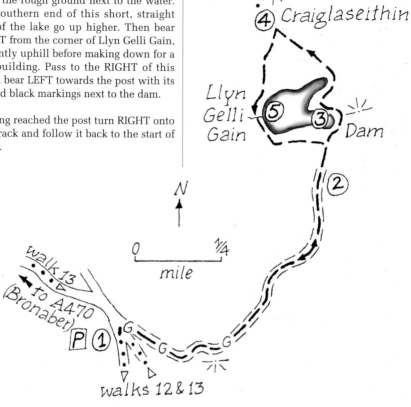

Craigaseithin from near Llyn Gelli Gain

WALK 12
LLECH IDRIS

DESCRIPTION A short walk which visits three sites of unusual historical interest. The walk starts at Pen y Stryd chapel, featured in the film on the life of Trawsfynydd's famous poet, Hedd Wyn, and once the focus for the religious life of the scattered settlements of the Gain valley. It then uses quiet roads and a well-made track to reach the ancient standing stone of Llech Idris, the grave of an early Christian and some Roman lime-kilns. Allow one hour.

START Parking space beside the chapel of Pen y Stryd (SH 726315).

DIRECTIONS From the A470 at Bronaber, two miles south of Trawsfynydd, take the minor road signposted for Llanuwchllyn, Abergeirw and the Trawsfynydd holiday village. Bear LEFT at the entrance to the village, then LEFT again to cross a cattle-grid. Pass the entrance to the Rhiwgoch Inn and artificial ski slope on the right, continuing uphill to pass Pen y Stryd farm on the left. Bear RIGHT just past the farm, go over a second cattle-grid and then immediately turn RIGHT to pass a stand of conifers before reaching Pen y Stryd chapel on the left. There is plenty of space to park next to the chapel.

I Bear LEFT from the car park, following the road past the chapel and graveyard. *There is immediately a marvellous view of the Gain valley to the left and of Craig y Penmaen (see* **Walk 13***) over to the right. Ahead, in the distance, you can see the ridge of Cadair Idris.* After a footpath sign the road begins to drop towards the lower Gain valley. Llech Idris comes into sight to your left and the farmhouse of Dol Gain to the right. Go LEFT through the metal gate opposite the track to Dol Gain and a footpath sign. *The track you are now on was built by the military who took over the Gain valley a century ago (see* **Walk 13***).*

2 After a short distance go RIGHT through a gate and down a field to Llech Idris. *Legend has it that Idris, the giant on Cadair Idris, threw the stone from the mountain. It travelled the 12 miles or so to land in this field.* Next to the stone there is a post with an arrow pointing up the field. Go uphill in the direction of the arrow to reach a stile. Cross the stile to return to the track and turn RIGHT, immediately going through a metal gate. The track then goes downhill and over a stream. Soon it crosses another stream before reaching a large, brick-built platform on the left, possibly used by the military as a loading bay. Pass the platform and then turn RIGHT onto a tarmac road.

3 The road goes downhill towards a stand of conifers and a bridge over the Gain. It bends first left and then right. At the point at which the road bears right, where there is a lay-by and entrance to a disused quarry on the left, go LEFT off the road and make for a rectangle of metal fencing about 300m away. The fencing surrounds the second of our objectives, Bedd Porius (shown as Porus on some maps). *This is a cast of the grave-stone of a man known as Porius. The original is in the National Museum at Cardiff and dates from about 700 AD. The Latin inscription, now partially obscured by moss and lichen, is usually translated as ' Porius lies here in the mound. He was a plain man'. Numbers on the stone were added by soldiers when this area was controlled by the military.*

4 Return to the road and turn RIGHT, going uphill and past the track along which you came originally. At a junction where a signpost indicates Trawsfynydd to the left and Llanuwchllyn to the right, go LEFT, continuing uphill to pass a waterpipe on the right. *This pipe is well known locally as a source of good drinking water.* Pass a footpath sign on the left as you continue uphill on the road. Then pass a stand of conifers on the left and a wood-yard on the right. Go ahead as the road levels off, passing the road to the chapel on your left and going over the cattle-grid.

5 Go RIGHT through a gate just past the cattle-grid and walk about 100m uphill, keeping to the right of the stream. You are

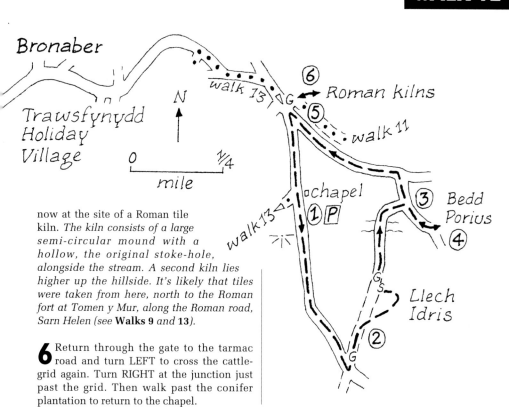

Bronaber

Trawsfynydd
Holiday
Village

N

0 ¼
mile

walk 13

⑥
Roman kilns
⑤
walk 11

chapel
①Ⓟ

③ Bedd
Porius
④

walk 13

G
S
Llech
Idris

②

G

now at the site of a Roman tile kiln. *The kiln consists of a large semi-circular mound with a hollow, the original stoke-hole, alongside the stream. A second kiln lies higher up the hillside. It's likely that tiles were taken from here, north to the Roman fort at Tomen y Mur, along the Roman road, Sarn Helen (see* **Walks 9** *and* **13***).*

6 Return through the gate to the tarmac road and turn LEFT to cross the cattle-grid again. Turn RIGHT at the junction just past the grid. Then walk past the conifer plantation to return to the chapel.

Llech Idris

WALK 13

ABOVE BRONABER

DESCRIPTION This short walk starts by the beautifully situated chapel of Pen y Stryd and climbs to join the Roman road which traverses the rocky and heather-covered slopes of Craig y Penmaen. On the return journey the Moelwyn mountains dominate the skyline to the north and there are glimpses of the settlement of Bronaber before you pass the farm of Pen y Stryd on your way back to the chapel. Allow 1½ hours.

START Parking space beside the chapel of Pen y Stryd (SH 726315).

DIRECTIONS From the A470 at Bronaber, two miles south of Trawsfynydd, take the minor road signposted for Llanuwchllyn, Abergeirw and the Trawsfynydd holiday village. Bear LEFT at the entrance to the village, then LEFT again to cross a cattle-grid. Pass the entrance to the Rhiwgoch Inn and artificial ski slope, continuing uphill to pass Pen y Stryd farm on the left. Bear RIGHT just past the farm, go over a second cattle-grid and then immediately turn RIGHT to pass a stand of conifers before reaching Pen y Stryd chapel on the left. There is plenty of space to park next to the chapel. (For information on the chapel see **Walk 12**).

1 Go through the gate opposite the parking space to follow a metalled track uphill. Soon go through a second gate before following the track round to the right to pass a military bunker before crossing a ridge. *The upper Gain valley, to your left, and the surrounding hills, were commandeered by the army, at the beginning of the 20th century. The inhabitants of the farms in the area were turned out of their homes which were reduced to ruins when used as targets for artillery practice. The army also commandeered the large, old house of Rhiwgoch and built a camp between it and the main Trawsfynydd to Dolgellau road (now the A470). The camp became known as Bronaber (after the farm of Aber below the road) or, more familiarly, as Tin Town since many of the army buildings were made of corrugated iron. The concrete bases of the buildings form the foundations of the holiday village chalets now on the site.*

2 Once over the ridge the track bends to the left and goes downhill to meet a track coming from the right. We will return to this point later. For now continue to the LEFT, making for the summit of Craig y Penmaen directly ahead. *The summit is named after Penmaen, a now-ruined farmhouse in the Gain valley below it. To the right of Craig y Penmaen, on the opposite side of the Eden valley below, is Y Garn (see **Walk 18**), an outlying peak of the Rhinogs. The track bends to the right and then left to avoid the high ground of Craig y Penmaen. Those who wish to climb to the summit should follow the wall on the left at the point at which the track goes right. When the first wall meets a second which curves down from the summit scramble up over some rocks and, keeping to its right, follow the second wall up until it begins to level off. Then go RIGHT to reach the summit which has two cairns separated by a jumble of rocks and heather. Soon the track goes through a gate to reach a rocky knoll below Craig y Penmaen. The knoll has good views and makes an excellent picnic spot. The track at this point follows the route of the Roman road, Sarn Helen, from the fort of Tomen y Mur in the north to that at Brithdir, near Dolgellau. A surviving stretch of the road can be seen above the farm of Pen y Stryd.*

3 Return the way you have come, following the track to the junction below the ridge. Bear LEFT at the junction to follow the grass-covered track downhill. *The track is now running parallel with the Rhinog ridge and provides excellent views of it from the high Diffwys (meaning 'precipice') in the south to the lower Diffwys at the end of the ridge in the north. The Moelwyns, above Blaenau Ffestiniog, can be clearly seen ahead. The track bears right uphill. At the top of the rise the wall on the left comes nearer and there is a rocky outcrop on the right. Go down to a metal gate with a stile to its left.*

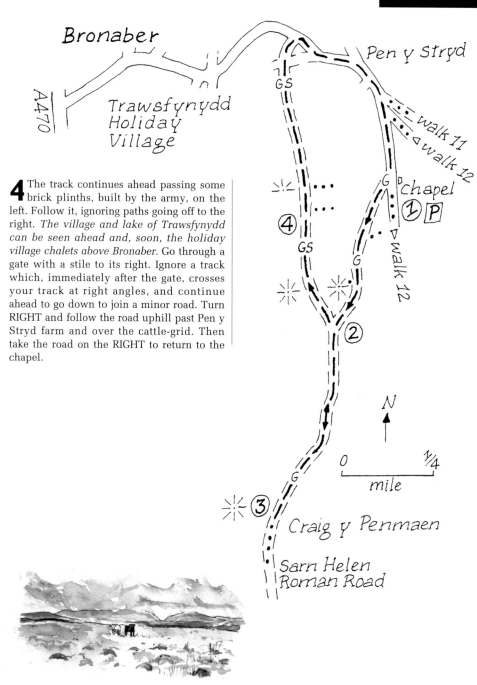

Bronaber

Pen y Stryd

A470

Trawsfynydd
Holiday
Village

GS

walk 11

walk 12

4 The track continues ahead passing some brick plinths, built by the army, on the left. Follow it, ignoring paths going off to the right. *The village and lake of Trawsfynydd can be seen ahead and, soon, the holiday village chalets above Bronaber.* Go through a gate with a stile to its right. Ignore a track which, immediately after the gate, crosses your track at right angles, and continue ahead to go down to join a minor road. Turn RIGHT and follow the road uphill past Pen y Stryd farm and over the cattle-grid. Then take the road on the RIGHT to return to the chapel.

chapel

① P

④

GS

② walk 12

N

0   ¼
mile

③

Craig y Penmaen

Sarn Helen
Roman Road

The Rhinog Ridge from near Craig y Penmaen

25

WALK 14

ABOVE TY'N Y GROES

DESCRIPTION This walk climbs to the remote house of Hafod y Fedw, high above the Ty'n y Groes pub in the Mawddach valley. It provides wonderful views of the valley and of the surrounding forest, Coed y Brenin, and then takes you through the remains of mine workings on the return. Allow 1½ hours.

START Parking space at the end of the minor road near Ty'n y Groes (SH 726226).

DIRECTIONS From the A470 about a mile south of Ganllwyd take the unsignposted minor road going uphill a short distance south of the Ty'n y Groes pub. The minor road winds steeply up and then through a gate. There is plenty of space to park at the road end.

1 Walk to the LEFT through a gateway and along a track which passes between sheep pens and a small, boarded-up house to a gate and marker. Once through, follow the track as it winds uphill, between walls and across a concreted-over waterpipe. Go through another gate and go RIGHT on the track, through trees and then down to a bridge over a stream. Cross this and then go RIGHT, ignoring an arrow pointing left, to follow a path steeply uphill and through a wall. The path goes through bracken to re-join the track which bends LEFT then RIGHT. Go ahead to the house you can see, which is Hafod y Fedw. *Hafod y Fedw is high but protected from the south-westerly winds by the low hills around it. From in front of it the view across the Mawddach valley to the east is dominated by the bulk of Rhobell Fawr.*

2 Pass to the RIGHT of the house, above its privy, and then go sharp LEFT behind it, between the house and barn. Ignore a track going down in front of the barn and follow the path going up a rocky slope to the RIGHT from the end of the house. Go on until your reach a point where a wall comes in from the left and there is a noticeboard on the right, next to an arrow pointing ahead. Turn LEFT here and go uphill to reach, after a short distance, a gully between low hills. Scramble up the rock and grass-covered hill on the LEFT to reach an excellent viewpoint. *From here you can see southwards down the Mawddach valley towards Llanelltyd, Dolgellau, and the cliffs and ridge of Cadair Idris. To the north the vast acreage of the conifers of Coed y Brenin becomes clear. You can also make out Ganllwyd and, above the village to the north, the Eden valley (see* **Walk 8***) and, to the north-east, the upper Mawddach valley.*

3 Return to the gully and then down to the notice-board and arrow. Turn LEFT here, following the winding path through a wall, passing a path coming in on the left. The path goes over a rocky knobble before making for a low, tumbledown wall and going over. Pass some fallen silver birches and go through another wall to emerge on a hillside above a stream, down to the right. The path makes its way to a gap in another wall. Go through and ahead, following the winding and undulating path until it climbs alongside a wall on the left to reach a weighted, metal gate between walls. The path then goes down by the wall on the left to a stream, then climbs again and bears RIGHT, going north away from the wall. It passes through bracken and soon goes gently downhill, bearing RIGHT and getting gradually closer to a wall on the right. Continue on the path until the point at which this wall goes off, initially sharply, to the right. Here, look ahead for a wooden post with a yellow top and make for it, passing a tree and crossing some boggy patches on the way. *As you walk this stretch of path you can make out the summits which feature on three other walks in this book. First, just to the right at the head of the Eden valley is the hump of Craig y Penmaen (***Walk 13***). Then, further to the right is the cone-shaped top of Craiglaseithin (***11***) and, further right still, the massive dome of Moel Oernant (***10***).*

4 Bear RIGHT at the post, following the path alongside a deeply-furrowed tractor track. The path joins the track which then goes downhill to a yellow marker. *Over to the right at this point you can see a shaft belonging to Cae Mawr, one of the mines in the Meirionnydd gold belt (see* **Walk 20***) which failed to produce any of the valuable metal. The workings extend downhill off to the right*

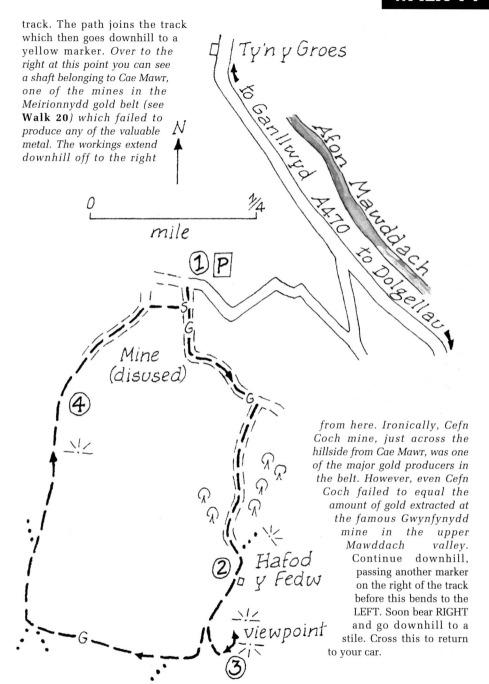

from here. *Ironically, Cefn Coch mine, just across the hillside from Cae Mawr, was one of the major gold producers in the belt. However, even Cefn Coch failed to equal the amount of gold extracted at the famous Gwynfynydd mine in the upper Mawddach valley.* Continue downhill, passing another marker on the right of the track before this bends to the LEFT. Soon bear RIGHT and go downhill to a stile. Cross this to return to your car.

WALK 15

ABOVE LLANELLTYD

DESCRIPTION A walk which takes you through forest and past a high lake before providing spectacular views across the Mawddach valley to Cadair Idris. At the end of the walk you go through the village of Llanelltyd, passing the church after which it is named. Allow 3½ hours.

START Side road just off the A470 in Llanelltyd (SH 718198).

DIRECTIONS Llanelltyd is just north of Dolgellau on the A470 and A496. From the roundabout just outside the village take the A470 north towards Porthmadog, pass the church on the right and take the next LEFT, a minor road which goes uphill past some houses. After a short distance turn LEFT where there is a no-through-road sign and park in this little used road.

1 Return to the minor road, turn LEFT and follow it uphill past a farm and a large house. Then turn RIGHT past a footpath sign on to a track. Go left of the padlocked gate and uphill through the forest. Soon, take the second of two paths coming downhill near each other on the LEFT and, after a steep climb, turn LEFT at a yellow marker. Cross a stream, turn RIGHT at a yellow marker, then immediately LEFT onto an uphill path. Soon this drops down to yellow markers at a junction of paths.

2 Turn RIGHT, alongside a wall, before going through a gap in it and uphill through cleared woodland. When the path levels off ignore a track to the right and go downhill to a forestry track and marker. Go RIGHT and, ignoring a path going ahead, follow the track LEFT uphill into the conifers. Soon self-seeded conifers cover parts of the track but continue ahead, following the line of it through some bog, over a stream and uphill. Soon you reach a track going uphill at right angles. Turn LEFT, going downhill past a yellow marker and a track on the right, then through a wall to a footpath sign and gate at the forest edge.

3 Turn RIGHT on to the road here, go through a gate, then turn LEFT onto a track and over a bridge. Follow the track through a wall towards a farmhouse with caravans, and then take the rough track which goes to the LEFT, before a stream, and down to a barn. Cross a stream and make for a yellow marker by some stone steps and a stile over the wall to the LEFT of the barn. Cross the wall and go half-LEFT towards three trees and an overhead power line. Go under the line, bear RIGHT and follow a grassy track through bracken to the LEFT of the trees. Bear LEFT by a stream and follow it down to some yellow markers. Cross the stream here, above a corrugated iron building, and go to the RIGHT, past a derelict JCB and uphill towards some piles of stones and another marker. Make for a small shed and some concrete posts, then for some markers on the other side of a track. Cross the track and take the path going downhill past the end of a moss-covered wall to another marker. Cross a stream on a wooden bridge to emerge from the trees. Go downhill towards a telegraph pole and then bear RIGHT, joining a track leading to a gate. Go over the stile to the left of the gate, cross the stream, and follow the path through the trees to a ruined building, passing it on the RIGHT. Cross a stream to reach a junction in the path and markers. Bear RIGHT here past a building with a corrugated iron roof and go uphill to bear RIGHT at another marker alongside a wall with conifers beyond. Continue uphill to reach a junction of four paths. Go LEFT downhill, then RIGHT when a path comes in from the left alongside an old wall. Go ahead to a gap in a wall and the lake beyond. *The lake is Llyn Tan y Graig, a reservoir from which Llanelltyd once drew its water supply.*

4 Turn LEFT along the dam at the end of the lake and cross a stile. Follow the path down to the LEFT, past a footpath sign and through gorse towards a stile by the forest wall. Bear RIGHT just before the stile to follow a fence to a gate and yellow markers.

Go through and bear RIGHT, following a path down to a wall. Bear RIGHT here, go over a stile and follow the path to a junction. Here, go LEFT downhill next to the wall and some ancient trees. Go through a wooden gate, then downhill to a metal gate (ignore the wooden gate on the left) and, beyond, a road. Turn LEFT onto the road and follow it through Llanelltyd, past the old post office and chapel. Then go between concrete bollards and turn LEFT, alongside a high wall by the A470. Pass the church and then go LEFT by a footpath sign and up some steps. Then turn RIGHT, going uphill to the starting point.

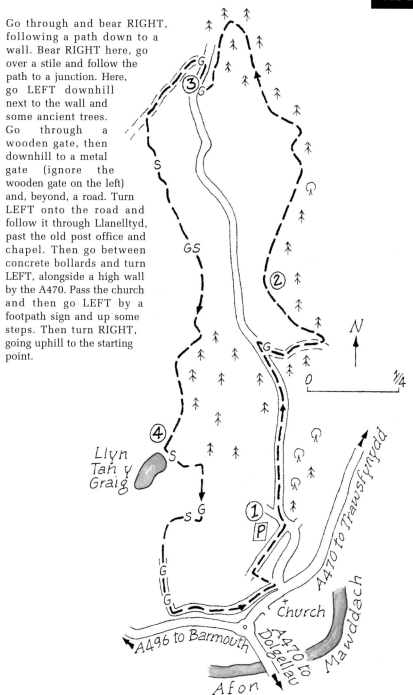

Llyn Tan y Graig

N

0   ¼

A470 to Trawsfynydd

A496 to Barmouth

Church

A470 to Dolgellau

Mawddach

Afon

WALK 16

DIFFWYS

DESCRIPTION A walk which climbs steeply from Cwm Mynach through derelict manganese workings to the summit of Diffwys. The walk then descends to join an old stage-coach road and crosses the Hirgwm valley to return to the starting point. Allow 6½ hours.

START Car park beside the Mynach valley map just to the north of the farm of Cwm Mynach Isaf (SH 684219).

DIRECTIONS Take the minor road going steeply uphill from the A496 at Taicynhaeaf (mid-way between Llanelltyd and Bontddu and opposite the minor road from the toll-bridge across the Mawddach at Penmaenpool). After passing through the village take the left-hand fork at a junction and continue uphill going through a gate. Go over a bridge and pass Cwm Mynach Isaf on the LEFT just before reaching a second gate. Go through and park in the space on the RIGHT next to the notice board just before the tarmac ends.

1 Go LEFT at the road end and uphill, bearing RIGHT at a junction. Continue ahead, eventually passing a footpath sign on the right. *Here the ridge of Diffwys and, on the other side of Cwm Mynach, the precipices below Y Garn (see **Walk 18**) are in sight.* Ignore a track on the left. Soon the track levels off and bends to the LEFT. When a derelict wall on the left intersects what appears to be a grass-covered wall, take a faint path going LEFT through the trees. The second wall is the base of a tramway from the manganese mines on Diffwys. Take care not to miss this path (about 35 minutes from the start). *Manganese was used to strengthen steel and the two Diffwys mines were some of the most extensive in the area.*

2 The path joins the tramway which goes through the trees to emerge near a stile. It then crosses a stream and goes into a gully, after which the tramway is, at times, elevated. It winds round a hillside, going west before turning sharply RIGHT, with a ruined wall directly ahead. Go uphill past

mine workings, onto a shale-covered slope, past a shaft entrance and into a gully. At the top of this, wind uphill through the workings and across a grassy slope to a wall. Turn LEFT and follow the wall uphill, keeping to the left of it and ignoring a stile before reaching the summit of Diffwys. *The view is stupendous, with Bardsey Island to the west, Anglesey and the peaks of Snowdonia to the north, Arenig, the Arans and the Berwyns to the east, and Cadair Idris to the south.*

3 Cross the stile by the cairn and go LEFT, following the wall down. Ignore a stile after about half a mile, go over a rise and down to another stile. Go LEFT over the wall here and follow a path downhill, parallel to a wall on the right. Make for a gateway and stile below in the valley, going through to pass a marker stone on the right. *You have now joined the old stage-coach road from Harlech to Dolgellau. This crosses the ridge below Diffwys from Pont Scethin.* Soon there is a second gateway and stile, followed by some wooden pathway posts. Continue down, bearing slightly LEFT of the wall you have been alongside. Ignore the path to the left, continuing ahead past a marker post. Go through a gate and past two wooden markers to reach the junction of the Harlech road with a drover's road from Talybont. *The junction has a large standing stone giving mileages to Harlech and Talybont.* Go LEFT, zig-zagging down a metal gate and tarmac road.

4 Turn LEFT, following the road downhill to a telephone box. Go LEFT through the gate just past this and follow the track uphill. The track then drops down to pass Ty'n y Cornel on the RIGHT of the house and the LEFT of the barn beyond it. Go through a gate at the barn end and then take a track which goes down to the LEFT. Immediately bear LEFT again, taking a pathway which crosses a stream and makes for a wall with a yellow-topped post and a

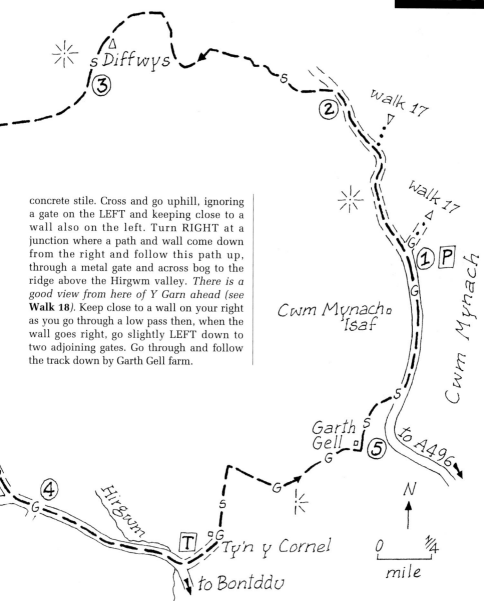

concrete stile. Cross and go uphill, ignoring a gate on the LEFT and keeping close to a wall also on the left. Turn RIGHT at a junction where a path and wall come down from the right and follow this path up, through a metal gate and across bog to the ridge above the Hirgwm valley. *There is a good view from here of Y Garn ahead (see* **Walk 18**). Keep close to a wall on your right as you go through a low pass then, when the wall goes right, go slightly LEFT down to two adjoining gates. Go through and follow the track down by Garth Gell farm.

5 Go LEFT here, following the track down to a yellow arrow on the left. Go LEFT between the trees to a second arrow, then half-RIGHT down to a third. Continue downhill through moss-covered rocks to a wall with another marker and a stone stile.

Cross, going ahead briefly and then over a ditch and RIGHT onto the path there. Cross a stile, turn LEFT and follow the road back to the start.

CWM MYNACH

DESCRIPTION A walk which passes Blaen Cwm Mynach, the remote house which is described in the book Four fields, five gates by Anne L. Hill before entering the forest which now carpets the valley. The walk then takes you on an old path which crosses the Afon Cwm Mynach by means of an isolated footbridge in the midst of the trees. The return journey is made on a track which was once used to gain access to the manganese mines on the shoulder of Diffwys, one of the mountains in the Rhinog range. Allow 1½ hours.

START Car park beside the Mynach valley map to the north of the farm of Cwm Mynach Isaf (SH 684219).

DIRECTIONS Take the minor road going steeply uphill from the A496 at Taicynhaeaf (mid-way between Llanelltyd and Bontddu and opposite the minor road from the toll-bridge across the Mawddach at Penmaenpool). After passing through the village take the left-hand fork at a junction and continue uphill going through a gate. Go over a bridge and pass Cwm Mynach Isaf on the LEFT just before reaching a second gate. Go through and park in the space on the RIGHT next to the notice board just before the tarmac ends.

1 Bear RIGHT at the end of the tarmac, going through a gate to pass Cwm Mynach Canol and its outbuildings on your right. Go over a stile by a gate and cross a bridge over the river. *The Canol bridge over the Cwm Mynach river is mentioned early in the book Four fields, five gates when the new tenants of Blaen Cwm Mynach take a car over it for the first time.* Follow the track, passing two large cypresses and then, when the track goes away from the river, look to the left for your first glimpse of Blaen Cwm Mynach. Soon the track is joined by a wall on the right and goes towards the house. Take the track which goes to the RIGHT before it and make for a stile and gate at the edge of the forest. *Pause to admire the view of Cadair Idris down the valley at this point. The two cypresses, the walled enclosures*

and green fields surrounding Blaen Cwm Mynach give the area a feel of parkland rather than sheep farm. It's certainly an idyllic spot. Four fields, five gates was first published half a century ago but was re-issued by John Jones in 1999. It tells of the trials, tribulations and triumphs of three women who rent the remote Blaen Cwm Mynach (or Blaen y Cwm as it is still called locally) during the 1940s. This was, of course, before the valley became covered in conifers and when it was possible to get to Penmaenpool, in the Mawddach estuary at the foot of Cwm Mynach, by train. The house had lain empty for 20 years before the women moved in to begin making it inhabitable once more. The book is full of amusing anecdotes and interesting detail. It also contains photographs of the house and valley as well as a map of the land surrounding the house.

2 Follow the track into the forest, bearing LEFT when a second track comes in from the right. Continue uphill, passing a footpath marker on the right before going LEFT into the trees at a marker and pile of boulders on the left. Keep alongside a tumbledown wall then when a rough track crosses the path go RIGHT through a gap and then LEFT downhill on the other side of the wall. Watch for orange ribbons in the trees; these are used consistently to mark the path. Go through the wall and back before the path meets a more stoutly built wall at right angles, beyond which is a clearing in the forest. Go LEFT then RIGHT through the new wall, then follow it downhill to the LEFT. When a stream comes in from the left cross it and go LEFT through a gap in the wall where there is a marker. Go down past a tree with a marker to reach a footbridge with a yellow marker on it.

3 Cross the bridge and go half-RIGHT uphill, scrambling over a fallen tree and crossing a tumbledown wall before going up alongside it. Follow the markers as the path goes away from the wall and soon you will arrive at a metal footpath post alongside a forestry track. *There is a good view of the end of the Diffwys ridge up to the right from* here (see **Walk 16**). *This part of Diffwys was the site of manganese mining and the mountain side is riddled with the remains of tramways and spoil heaps. Manganese was used in the strengthening of steel and as many as 12 mines were opened in Meirionnydd during 1886 alone.*

4 Turn LEFT onto the track and follow it downhill, passing the remains of a large farm settlement on the left. When the track divides go LEFT downhill to return to the starting point.

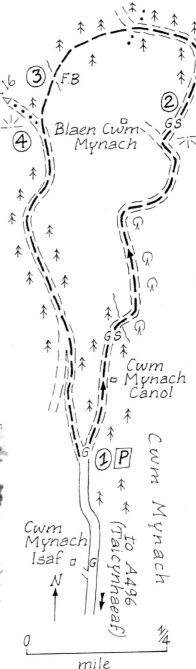

Blaen Cwm Mynach with its view to Cadair Idris

33

WALK 18

Y GARN

DESCRIPTION This walk takes you to the summit of a comparatively little known mountain but one which provides magnificent views of the Rhinog ridge and Cadair Idris. The climb takes you past the farmhouse of Cesailgwm Mawr to a ridge high above the Mynach valley before you cross a wild plateau to the summit cairn of Y Garn. If you opt to walk down the mountain's southern ridge this offers a spectacular panorama of the Mawddach estuary. Allow 3½ hours.

START Parking just off the minor road below Cesailgwm Mawr (SH 696205).

DIRECTIONS Take the minor road going steeply uphill from the A496 at Taicynhaeaf (mid-way between Llanelltyd and Bontddu and opposite the minor road from the toll-bridge across the Mawddach at Penmaenpool). After passing through the village take the right-hand fork, marked 'New Precipice Walk', at a junction and continue uphill going over a cattle-grid. Bear RIGHT at the next junction, go over a bridge and through a gate. There are several car-parking spaces off the road above the gate.

I Return through the gate, take the first RIGHT and walk up to Cesailgwm Mawr. Go through the gate before the house, turn LEFT immediately through a second gate and then go RIGHT across a field and over a stream making for a gate in the far RIGHT corner. *There are usually llamas in this field; they are inquisitive but harmless.* Go through and turn LEFT on a track going towards a barn. Ignore a gate on the right and, just before the barn gate, go RIGHT over a stile and up to a track. Go RIGHT, go alongside a fence and then up LEFT through a gate. Follow a path which soon goes slightly LEFT through heather. Go LEFT onto a track and follow this uphill, ignoring another track going left. After a gate, the track bends away from the conifers on your right. Eventually, it levels off just before you reach a grassy slope going up through heather on the RIGHT.

2 Go up the slope, past a ruin. When the grass peters out follow a faint path through the heather towards the trees. Go LEFT uphill alongside the wall and fence by the conifers. When a wall comes in from the left cross a high stone stile over it. Continue uphill by the trees. Go RIGHT alongside the topmost edge of the conifers, then immediately turn LEFT and scramble up to the small cairn on the ridge above.

3 The summit of Y Garn can now be seen half-RIGHT and, nearer, its lower summit of Garn Fach. Make for the latter, going ahead on the ridge and then bearing RIGHT towards it, crossing low hills with no clear path. From the summit of Garn Fach make for Y Garn keeping to the LEFT on the highest ground. Climb the steep hillside below the summit, keeping LEFT of the cliffs to the south. The summit is a rocky knoll with a cairn. *The view from Y Garn is dominated by the Rhinog ridge. Snowdon can be seen to the north, Arenig and the Arans to the east, Cadair Idris south and the Mawddach estuary west.*

4 *From the summit of Y Garn you should retrace your steps via Garn Fach and Cesailgwm Mawr to your car. The return via the south ridge of Y Garn set out below is not advised since it involves stepping over a wall.* Go south towards Cadair Idris from the summit, following a faint path down through a shallow gully to a wall going ahead along the ridge down from Y Garn. Keep LEFT of this wall and go RIGHT across it above the tiny lake of Nannau is Afon. Continue downhill on the path on the RIGHT of the wall. Go LEFT through a gate in the ridge wall when another wall joins it from the right. Then go downhill bearing slightly LEFT away from the ridge wall towards a gate in a wall coming in from the left near where the ridge levels off. Go through and bear RIGHT to go through a gate in the ridge wall. Then go LEFT and follow the wall along the ridge, ignoring a faint track which goes to the right. Keep near to the wall as you go downhill on rough ground, eventually passing a ruined house over the wall on the left before you reach a stile. Go

LEFT over the stile and LEFT again to follow the wall the short distance back to the ruin.

5 Standing at the front of the ruin look for a gate in the distance, directly ahead and to the LEFT of a small lake. Make for the gate by going half-LEFT from the house and skirting the bog in front of it by walking along the foot of the gorse-covered hillside on the LEFT. Go over a rise, across a stream and through the gate to join the track beyond. Turn RIGHT and go through a gap in a wall. Follow the track gently uphill and through a gully past a cairn on the LEFT. Soon the track bears LEFT and goes over a low ridge next to mine workings. Go through a gate, and follow the track round to the RIGHT. Go through another gate, past a barn, through a gateway and down to a wall. Go over a stile when the track bears left away from the wall and follow the wall down to a gate and road. Turn RIGHT through the gate and follow the road downhill. Soon, go through a gate to return to the starting point.

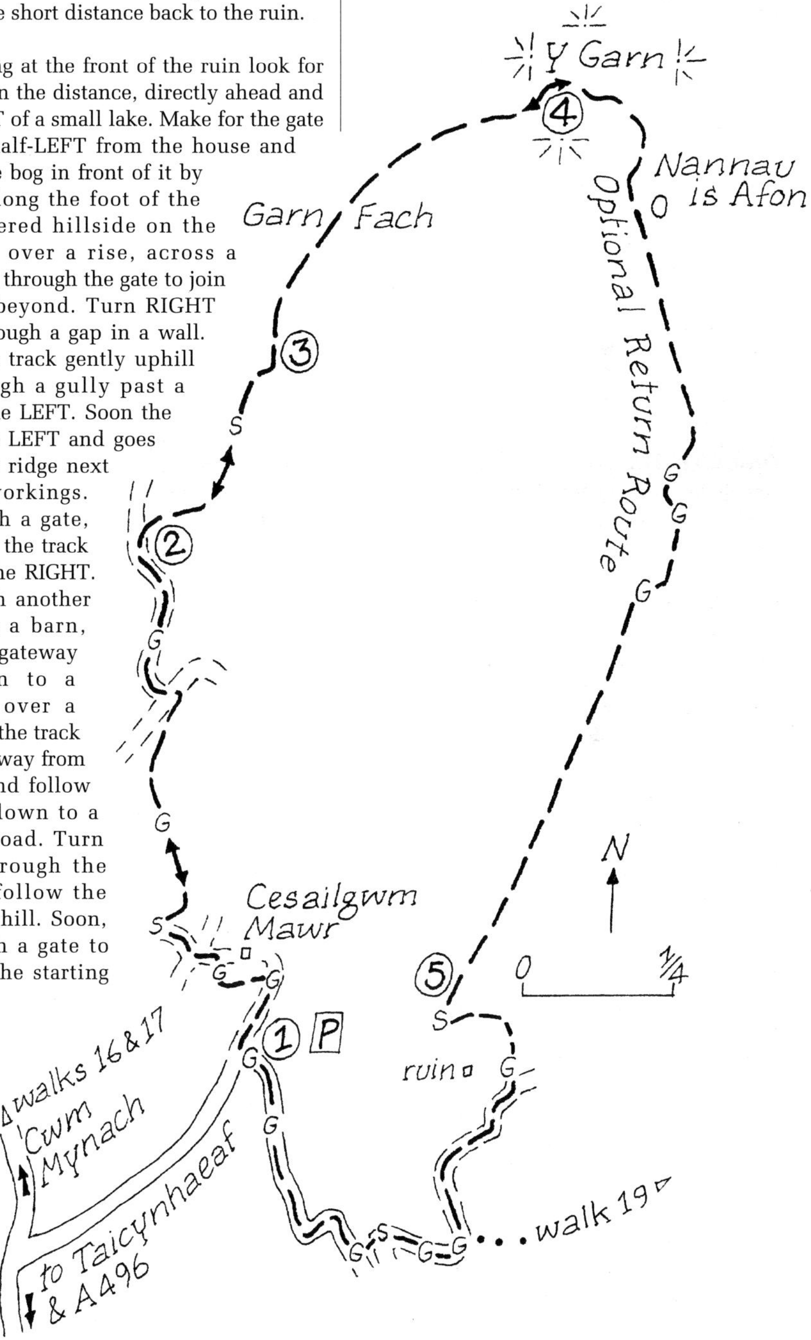

Y Garn

Garn Fach

Nannau is Afon

Optional Return Route

③

②

N

Cesailgwm Mawr

⑤

① P

ruin

▲ walks 16 & 17

Cwm Mynach

to Taicynhaeaf & A496

...walk 19

0   ¼

WALK 19

FOEL ISPRI

DESCRIPTION A walk which provides panoramic views of the Mawddach Estuary and Cadair Idris for very little effort. It takes you along part of the New Precipice Walk, passes gold mine workings and visits the summit of Foel Ispri, one of the most conspicuous high points in the Dolgellau area. Allow 1½ hours.

START Off-road parking just below Foel Ispri Uchaf (SH698201).

DIRECTIONS Take the minor road going steeply uphill from the A496 at Taicynhaeaf (mid-way between Llanelltyd and Bontddu and opposite the minor road from the toll-bridge across the Mawddach at Penmaenpool). After passing through the village take the right-hand fork, marked 'New Precipice Walk', at a junction and continue uphill going over a cattle-grid. Bear RIGHT at the next junction, go over a bridge and through two gates. When the road bends sharply LEFT next to a ruined building go ahead for a short distance and park off the road on a grassy space on the RIGHT below a wall and footpath sign.

I Walk up the road, bearing RIGHT and through a metal gate to follow a newly made path in front of Foel Ispri Uchaf. After the house join a track going to the RIGHT, following it through a gate and then across the steep slope below Foel Ispri. *There are magnificent views from here both of the Mawddach Estuary, with the George Inn and toll bridge tiny specks below, and Cadair Idris towering above you on the opposite side of the valley.* When you go through a gap in a wall ignore the track which goes down to some ruined buildings and bear LEFT to cross a tramway and pass the spoil heaps of the first of the Foel Ispri mine workings. *Amongst the ruins below there was a blacksmith's shop and there is a shaft on the right of the path. The spoil heaps above you to the left are a reminder of the large volume of earth, rock and rubble which was shifted in the search for often minute quantities of gold.*

2 Follow the path as it goes across a stream and uphill through grass and bracken to pass through a gap in a wall. Continue ahead on the path, ignoring minor branches to left or right, to reach a junction where you should bear LEFT. This path crosses a low ridge, passing some piles of stones, drops down to cross a boggy patch and then goes gently up between two rocks to reach a track at right angles. Bear LEFT along this track, noting a small lake down to your left and a single, small tree on the ridge of Foel Ispri above it. Follow the track up and then downhill, bearing LEFT to go through a gap in a wall. *There is a good view of the Rhinog Ridge over to the right from here. Closer at hand in the same direction is a third, even smaller, lake and a ruined house which can be reached by going through the wooden gate on the right.*

to Taicynhaeaf & A496

3 Continue ahead, following the track which goes gently uphill and through a gully past a cairn on the LEFT. *There is soon a magnificent view ahead down the Mawddach Estuary to the sea. Barmouth railway bridge can be made out in clear conditions.* Soon the track bears LEFT and over a low ridge with mine workings above it on the left. Leave the track at this point and go LEFT to reach the mine entrance. Continue uphill just to the RIGHT of the entrance and you will find a fenced-off shaft forming part of the same mine workings. You are now on the summit ridge of Foel Ispri. Facing Cadair Idris, go down, half-LEFT from the shaft to cross a stile and reach the summit's triangulation station. *Foel Ispri is over 320m in height and its triangulation station is, unusually, not on the highest point of the ridge. The view ranges from Rhobell Fawr and the Aran mountains in the east to Cardigan Bay in the west. To the north of Foel Ispri you can see much of the Rhinog ridge, with Diffwys dominating the skyline in front of you. And, below, the confluence of the Mawddach with the*

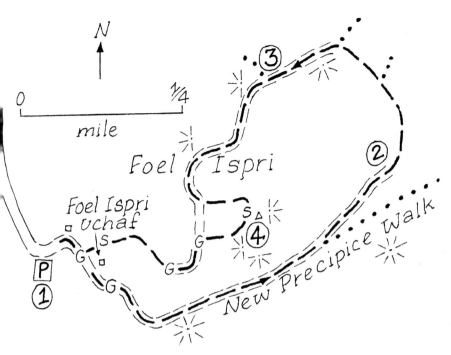

N
↑

0 ——————————————— ¼
          mile

Foel Ispri

Foel Ispri uchaf

New Precipice Walk

Wnion, which flows through Dolgellau, can be seen. Notice, too, the extent of the earthworks designed to minimise flooding. Until the 1960s, trains ran through the estuary travelling betweeen Dolgellau and Barmouth. The disused line has been turned into a foot and cycle path, and can be seen, straight as a ruler, crossing the marshland to the west of the George Inn and toll-bridge.

4 Return to the stile but, instead of crossing it, turn LEFT and follow the fence downhill to a metal gate. Here, rejoin the track you left earlier and follow it as it sweeps round to the RIGHT and through a gate. Go past a barn, through a gateway and down to a wall. Go over a stile at the point where the track bears left away from the wall and follow the wall down to a metal gate and tarmac road. Turn RIGHT through the gate and follow the road down to the starting point.

Penmaenpool Station c. 1925

WALK 20
ABOVE BONTDDU

DESCRIPTION This walk takes you through an idyllic valley high above the Mawddach estuary. It passes a gold mine, provides good views of the estuary and of Cadair Idris, and returns along a path next to the fast-flowing waters of the Afon Hirgwm. Allow 1½ hours.

START Parking space opposite the phone box near Llechfraith (SH668198).

DIRECTIONS Bontddu is mid-way between Dolgellau and Barmouth on the A496. Take the minor road going steeply uphill from the Bontddu Hall Hotel (on the RIGHT coming from Dolgellau) near the centre of the village. The road goes over a cattle-grid and past several houses before reaching a telephone box at a junction. Park in the space on the LEFT next to a footpath sign.

1 Go through the gate opposite and follow the track uphill. *Look over to the left as you get higher for a good view of the cliffs of Diffwys, the southernmost peak of the main Rhinog ridge (see* **Walk 16***).* The track then drops down to pass Ty'n y Cornel on the RIGHT of the house and the LEFT of the barn beyond it. Go through a gate at the barn end and follow the track going uphill ahead of you. After a short distance you will reach a stone building with corrugated iron roof on your left. Here, turn sharp RIGHT to reach an entrance to the upper levels of Clogau gold mine. *The tram-line into Clogau is still in place and one of the trucks used in the mine has been positioned beyond the locked metal-grill entrance gate. The St David's Lode of Clogau was one of the most productive in the area and, indeed, was so successful during 1862 that it provoked a gold rush to Meirionnydd. Gold was found at Clogau in 1853 and the mine was worked on a large scale until early in the 20th Century. It is one of four important mines in the Meirionnydd gold belt which stretches from near Bontddu to the Prince Edward Mine near Trawsfynydd (see* **Walk 9***).*

2 Return to the gate by the barn at Ty'n y Cornel, turn round and then take a second track which goes down to the LEFT towards some mine workings. Immediately bear LEFT again, taking a pathway which crosses a stream and makes for a wall where there is a yellow-topped post, and stone and concrete stile. Once over this, go uphill, ignoring a gate on the LEFT and keeping close to a wall also on the left. Bear LEFT at a junction where a path and wall come down from the right and continue ahead between the two walls. Cross a stream and pass a wooden gate in the wall on your left. Immediately after this bear RIGHT to go over an old slab bridge over the Afon Cwm Llechen, one of whose tributaries flows down from the summit ridge of Diffwys. Bear LEFT to re-join the track which fords the river below the bridge and go uphill to a metal gate with a stile to its left. The track continues uphill alongside a wall on the left then levels off and reaches a wooden gate, again with a stile on the left. After this, go uphill on the track and through a stream to reach a locked metal gate and stile, beyond which is a tarmac road. *Down to the left there is a good view of the Mawddach below Bontddu, with Cadair Idris towering above the estuary to the south.*

3 Go over the stile and straight ahead on the road, immediately passing through a gate and then going uphill. Pass a yellow marker sign and, when you reach a junction alongside a roofless barn, take the grassy track going downhill to the LEFT alongside a wall. Follow the track, now with a concreted surface, through a gate with a yellow marker, and then to a stile over the wall on the left where there is a footpath sign. Go over the stile, bear LEFT and then immediately RIGHT over another stile into woodland. Turn LEFT at a yellow arrow just over the stile and go downhill, keeping fairly close to the fence on the left. Bear LEFT as the Hirgwm comes into sight and follow the path down past a metal gate on the left and across a stream where there is a yellow marker. To avoid losing the path at this stage, go ahead, not downhill to the right as the marker seems to indicate, keeping close the fence on your left to reach a stile over a wall.

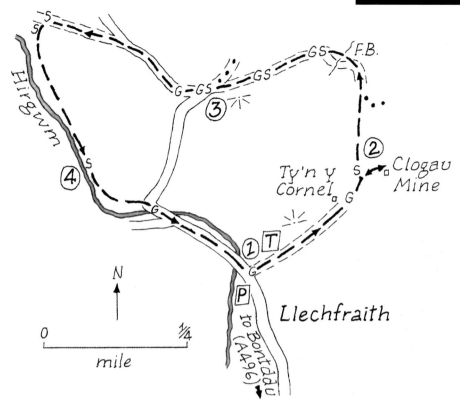

4 The path bears down towards the river alongside a fence on the left. *The Hirgwm is just over to the right at this point and can easily be reached. The river is spectacular after heavy rain.* Pass an empty reservoir, on the right, before the path reaches a tarmac road. Go ahead onto the road, following it down to a gate and bridge over the river. Go through the gate and uphill to turn LEFT at a road junction. Go downhill to reach the starting point.

The entrance to the Clogau Mine, near Ty'n y Cornel – early 1900s

PRONUNCIATION

These basic points should help non-Welsh speakers

Welsh	English equivalent
c	always hard, as in cat
ch	as in the Scottish word loch
dd	as th in then
f	as v in vocal
ff	as f
g	always hard as in got
ll	no real equivalent. It is like 'th' in then, but with an 'L' sound added to it, giving 'thlan' for the pronunciation of the Welsh 'Llan'.

. In Welsh the accent usually falls on the last-but-one syllable of a word.

KEY TO THE MAPS

- ➡ Walk route and direction
- ═ Metalled road
- ‒‒‒ Unsurfaced road
- •••• Footpath/route adjoining walk route
- ∿ River/stream
- ♠ ♤ Trees
- ▰▰ Railway
- **G** Gate
- **S** Stile
- ☼ Viewpoint
- Ⓟ Parking
- Ⓣ Telephone

THE COUNTRY CODE

Enjoy the countryside and respect its life and work

Guard against all risk of fire

Leave gates *as you find them*

Keep your dogs under close control

Keep to public paths across farmland

Use gates and stiles to cross fences, hedges and walls

Leave livestock, crops and machinery alone

Take your litter home

Help to keep all water clean

Protect wildlife, plants and trees

Take special care on country roads

Make no unnecessary noise

Published by
Kittiwake
3 Glantwymyn Village Workshops,
Cemmaes Road, Machynlleth, Montgomeryshire
SY20 8LY

© Text & maps (from ooc base): Michael Burnett 2004
© Illustrations: Kittiwake 2004

Main cover photograph: Rhobell-y-big, with the Rhinogs behind: Myrddyn Phillips.
Inset photograph: Bontddu Hall, near Barmouth
© Wales Tourist Board 2004

Care has been taken to be accurate. However neither the author nor the publisher can accept responsibility for any errors which may appear, or their consequences. If you are in doubt about any access, check before you proceed.

Printed on ❧ eVolution recycled paper by WPG, Welshpool, Powys

ISBN: 1 902302 30 3